Especially for

_____

From

_____

Date

_____

Blissful Moments
for Women

{ Refreshing Moments for Your Soul }

BARBOUR
PUBLISHING

ISBN 978-1-60260-812-2

Devotional readings are from *365 Daily Whispers of Wisdom for Busy Women*, published by Barbour Publishing, Inc.

Prayers by Jackie M. Johnson are from *Power Prayers for Women*, published by Barbour Publishing, Inc.

Scripture quotations marked CEV are from the Contemporary English Version, Copyright © 1991, 1992, 1995 by American Bible Society. Used by permission.

Scripture quotations marked NASB are taken from the New American Standard Bible, © 1960, 1962, 1963, 1968, 1971, 1972, 1973, 1975, 1977, 1995 by The Lockman Foundation. Used by permission.

Scripture quotations marked MSG are from *THE MESSAGE*. Copyright © by Eugene H. Peterson 1993, 1994, 1995, 1996, 2000, 2001, 2002. Used by permission of NavPress Publishing Group.

Scripture quotations marked KJV are taken from the King James Version of the Bible.

Scripture quotations marked NIV are taken from the HOLY BIBLE, NEW INTERNATIONAL VERSION®. NIV®. Copyright © 1973, 1978, 1984 by International Bible Society. Used by permission of Zondervan. All rights reserved.

Scripture quotations marked NKJV are taken from the New King James Version®. Copyright © 1982 by Thomas Nelson, Inc. Used by permission. All rights reserved.

Cover and interior illustration: Todd Williams

Published by Barbour Publishing, Inc., P.O. Box 719, Uhrichsville, Ohio 44683, www.barbourbooks.com

Our mission is to publish and distribute inspirational products offering exceptional value and biblical encouragement to the masses.

 Member of the
Evangelical Christian
Publishers Association

Printed in China.

CONTENTS

INTRODUCTION

AHH, BLISS!

*[Jesus] said. . ."Come with me by
yourselves to a quiet place and get some rest."*
MARK 6:31 NIV

No doubt about it, those much-longed-for *"ahh. . ."* moments
are few and far between. Take a minute to revive and refresh your
harried soul with these bliss-filled scriptures, quotations, and
prayers that will invite you to rest and reflect upon the everyday
things that sweeten your life and bring you a little closer to God.

Blessings

God can pour on the
blessings in astonishing ways.

2 CORINTHIANS 9:8 MSG

A LITTLE TIME WITH GOD

Susan headed out of her house in the same way she always did—in a hurry, guiding two children before her, double-checking their backpacks as she went and reminding them of chores and practices scheduled for that afternoon. "Remember, 3:30 is ballet; 4:00 is soccer. I'll pick you up school, but I have to go back to work, so—"

She stopped as her coat snagged on a bush. "What?—" She looked down to find her hem caught firmly by a cluster of thorns. As she stooped to untangle the cloth, the stem bent suddenly, and Susan found herself nose-to-petal with a rose. It smelled glorious, and she paused, laughing.

When Susan had planted the bush, a friend had asked why. "You never stop long enough to enjoy even what God drops in front of you. What makes you think you'll care about a rose?"

Susan glanced up toward the sky. "Thanks for grabbing me. I guess I should spend a little more time with You."

God blesses us every day in both great and simple ways. Children, friends, work, faith—all these things form a bountiful buffet of gifts, and caring for them isn't always enough. We need to spend a little time with the One who has granted us the blessings.

~Ramona Richards

As God loveth a cheerful giver, so He also loveth a cheerful taker. . .who takes hold on His gifts with a glad heart.

JOHN DONNE

GOD WILL PROVIDE

*L*ord, I thank You for providing for my
needs. I give You my worries and fears—those
nagging thoughts about lacking money for
clothes, food, and the basics of life. You feed
the sparrows in the field, Lord—You'll certainly
help me and my family. Your resources are
limitless—You have an abundance of blessings.
I praise You for Your goodness, Lord, and the
faithfulness of Your provision.

~Jackie M. Johnson

*"Give thanks to God. . . . Shout to the
nations, tell them what he's done,
spread the news of his great reputation!"*

Isaiah 12:3 MSG

GIVE THANKS

Common courtesy grows more uncommon in our society with the passing of each generation. Finding someone who puts others first and uses words like *please* and *thank you* is like finding a rare gem. Most people hurry to their next task with little thought of others crossing their paths.

Every favor and earthly blessing that we experience is given to us by God. It is nothing we have accomplished in our own right. All that God has done since the beginning of creation, He did for humankind. You are His greatest treasure.

Give thanks to God today for giving you life—the very air you breathe. He has given you the ability to make a living, to feed your family, and to give to others. He is a good Father—He won't withhold anything good from you.

What has God done for you lately? What doors of opportunity has He opened? Give Him the credit, tell others of His goodness, and thank Him! It blesses God to hear you express your gratitude, and it will do your heart good as well.

~Shanna D. Gregor

When we start to count flowers,
we cease to count weeds;
When we start to count blessings,
we cease to count needs;
When we start to count laughter,
we cease to count tears;
When we start to count memories,
we cease to count years.

UNKNOWN

LIVING WELL

$\mathcal{L}$ord, when I think of "living well," help me to be drawn toward Your ways, not the world's. Show me the difference between what I want and what I really need. Help me to know that my true success lies in being right in love, wealthy in good works toward others, and generous in sharing from Your abundant blessing. I thank You for the prosperity You provide, inside and out.

–Jackie M. Johnson

Whatever is true, whatever is noble,
whatever is right, whatever is pure,
whatever is lovely, whatever is admirable—
if anything is excellent or praiseworthy—
think about such things.

PHILIPPIANS 4:8 NIV

Conversation

*Be gracious in your speech.
The goal is to bring out the best in
others in a conversation.*

<small>COLOSSIANS 4:6 MSG</small>

WALK AND PRAY

*T*heir friendship began when their daughters played on the same soccer team. Leaning against their cars, they chatted and waited for practice to end, both realizing after a couple of conversations that they had more in common than two energetic thirteen-year-old girls. They shared a common faith in God, and both women were experiencing the growing pains that come with parenting adolescents.

One day the women decided to start wearing their workout gear to practice so that they could talk and pray for their daughters as they walked the perimeter of the soccer field. By the end of the season, both women were encouraged and strengthened, and they had forged a deep friendship. The added bonus was their increased fitness levels derived from these long walks.

Jesus said, "For where two or three come together in my name, there am I with them" (Matthew 18:20 NIV). Real power is available when friends get together for fellowship and prayer, because Christ Himself is right there with them. Along with gaining another's insight and perspective, anytime we share a burden with a friend, our load instantly becomes lighter.

Is there a friend you might call today to join you in a prayer walk?

~Austine Keller

The sweetest conversation between friends is the silent communication of their hearts.

BONNIE JENSEN

REACHING OUT
TO OTHERS

*L*ord, would You please show me how I can reach out to someone who needs a friend? Bring to mind people with whom I can share the love of Christ. Let my words and actions reflect Your love, acceptance, and compassion. Give me eyes to see the needs and a heart to respond. As I look out for the needs of others, and not just my own, I pray that I would be a vessel of Your blessing and joy.

~Jackie M. Johnson

Watch the way you talk. . . .
Say only what helps, each word a gift.

Ephesians 4:29 MSG

WELL-SEASONED SPEECH

Cassie was a horrible cook! Her food was bland, flat, and boring to the extreme—no zest, no zing to tempt you for a second helping. Oh, she'd try to please people with what they wanted, but the result was pathetic.

As pale and uninviting as Cassie's food was, her conversations were the exact opposite: full of life, spiced with the hope of the gospel, meaty with truth, and sprinkled with kindness and love. People were drawn to her and would linger in conversation, savoring the sweet aroma of Christ that bubbled from within her. She didn't preach or use Christianese. Instead, she used words that encouraged, challenged, or piqued you for more. When asked about this, she admitted to making every effort to choose words that build up people, make them laugh, or give truths to chew on when they walk away—a practice of longer-lasting value than cuisine acclaim.

—P. J. Lehman

*There are few things in life as
encouraging as the voice of a friend.
It's not just the words they speak,
but the gentle way they convey them.*

BONNIE JENSEN

BEING A BETTER LISTENER

Lord, I praise You today for all You have done for me. You have brought help, hope, healing, and restoration, and I want to tell people! Help me proclaim Your goodness, sharing the amazing ways You have come through for me. But as I speak, help me to be a good listener, too. Through Your Spirit, Lord, may I show I care about my friends. Give me wisdom to know when my ears should be open and my mouth shut.

~Jackie M. Johnson

May our Lord Jesus Christ. . .
encourage your hearts and strengthen
you in every good deed and word.

2 THESSALONIANS 2:16—17 NIV

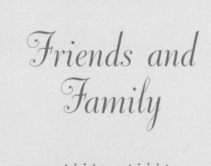

Friends and
Family

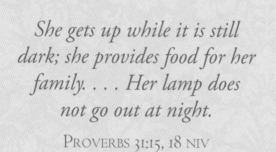

She gets up while it is still dark; she provides food for her family. . . . Her lamp does not go out at night.

UNIQUELY WIRED

The Proverbs 31 woman puts Wonder Woman to shame. Up before dawn, late to bed, caring for her household, negotiating business contracts down at the city gate. . . She gives to the poor, plans for her household to run smoothly, anticipates future needs, such as snowy weather. Even her arms are buff! "She sets about her work vigorously; her arms are strong for her tasks" (Proverbs 31:17 NIV).

She is highly energetic, an efficiency expert, and gifted in relationships. "Her children arise and call her blessed; her husband also, and he praises her" (v. 28). This woman is downright intimidating!

So how do we benefit by reading about the Proverbs 31 woman? Reading about her day makes us feel overwhelmed, discouraged by our inadequacies. That bar is too high!

God doesn't place the bar so high that we live in its shadow. He wired each of us with different gifts, different energy levels, different responsibilities. Proverbs 31 casts a floodlight on all women—those gifted in business, in home life, as caregivers. This chapter displays how women undergird their families and their communities.

Remember, the book of Proverbs was written in the tenth century BC, when women were considered chattel. But not in God's eyes. He has always esteemed women and the many roles we fulfill in society.

~Suzanne Woods Fisher

So much of what is great has sprung from the closeness of family ties.

James M. Barrie

UNCONDITIONAL LOVE

*L*ord, I thank You for my family members and those who are like family to me. I am grateful for their love and understanding. May I be loving in return—not only with those who love me, but even with those who are hard to be around. Your ways are merciful and kind, forgiving and good. Help me to reflect Your love, finding joy in loving others as You love me.

– Jackie M. Johnson

I know that nothing is better for them than to rejoice, and to do good in their lives, and also that every man should eat and drink and enjoy the good of all his labor—it is the gift of God.

Ecclesiastes 3:12–13 nkjv

Calmer Mind...
Grateful Heart

*W*omen today work hard—sometimes the labor seems endless. We care for our homes, families, employers, and churches. We cook, sort, haul, clean, and nurture, and that's before we even leave for our jobs outside the home. We run errands at lunch and often eat more meals behind the steering wheel than at the dinner table. Our days start early and end late, and we head for our beds as if sleep were a luxury instead of a necessity.

Yet constant work is not what God intended for our lives. We should work hard, yes, but not to the exclusion of rest and times of renewal for our minds and souls. As the author of Ecclesiastes points out, our work and the results of it—our food, homes, and friendships—are gifts that God meant for us to enjoy and appreciate.

Finding time isn't always easy, but the rewards of a calmer mind and a grateful heart will be well worth the effort.

– Ramona Richards

The secret of a full and happy life is to wake up every morning with the intention of doing as much as we can to nurture the friendships God has given us. In no time at all the joy will begin to pour in. . .and our days will be filled with His goodness.

BONNIE JENSEN

THANK YOU FOR MY FRIENDSHIPS

*L*ord, I thank You for my wonderful friends! As I think about the treasure chest of my close friends, casual friends, and acquaintances, I am grateful for the blessings and the joys each one brings to my life. Thank You for my "heart" friends, my loyal sister friends who listen, care, and encourage me. They are my faithful companions. I acknowledge that You, Lord, are the giver of all good gifts, and I thank You for Your provision in my friendships.

-Jackie M. Johnson

Friends love through all kinds of weather,
and families stick together in
all kinds of trouble.

PROVERBS 17:17 MSG

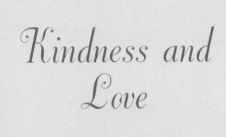

Kindness and
Love

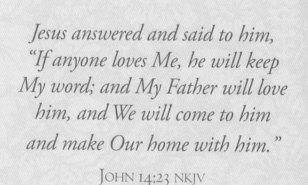

*Jesus answered and said to him,
"If anyone loves Me, he will keep
My word; and My Father will love
him, and We will come to him
and make Our home with him."*

JOHN 14:23 NKJV

Basic Math

*I*f you disliked math in school, perhaps at some point you asked, *How will I ever use it in real life?*

A certain kind of relational math is fundamental to your daily life. The words and actions exchanged throughout your day add to or take away from your life and the lives of those around you. Are you a positive or negative force? Are those around you positive or negative influences in your life?

God's nature is to give—to add—to every life He encounters. As Christians, we are created in His image and should be positive influences on those around us each day. Look around you and determine who adds to your life and who takes away. You will probably find that you prefer to spend time with pleasant communicators. Words of anger, frustration, confusion, and jealousy take away from the spirit of a man, but words of affirmation and gestures of kindness add to every heart.

Think before you act. Consider your words before you speak. Will you be adding to that person or taking away with what you are about to say or do? Share the love God shows you with others.

– Shanna D. Gregor

A kind heart is a fountain of gladness, making everything in its vicinity freshen into smiles.

WASHINGTON IRVING

THE REWARD

*Y*ou promise me wonderful rewards when I am charitable, Lord. I will be "like a watered garden, and like a spring of water, whose waters fail not" (Isaiah 58:11 KJV). Good health will come to me, as well as good reputation, and I will live a life of righteousness. Remind me of this the next time I pass up a charity event for an evening in front of the television set or hang up the telephone without even listening to the caller. I cannot answer every request made of me, so I count on You to guide me as to where I should invest my efforts in such as way as to bring You glory.

– Toni Sortor

"Arise, shine, for your light has come,
and the glory of the Lord rises upon you."

ISAIAH 60:1 NIV

REFLECTIONS OF LIGHT

God said, "Light, be," and light came into existence. Light appeared from the lips of God so He could see all He was about to create—and His creation could see Him.

When you gave your heart to God, His light came on inside your heart. Christianity lives from the inside out. When your heart is right, then your actions truly portray the influence that God and His Word have in your life.

Your life should then begin to reflect the character and nature of the One who created you and oppose all darkness. You are a reflection of His light to everyone around you. From within, you shine on the lives of others around you and become a light to the world.

As you point others to God, to His light—His goodness, mercy, and love—your light shines, repelling darkness and giving comfort to everyone God brings across your path.

How encouraging to know your life can brighten the whole room. You have the power to open the door of people's hearts for the Holy Spirit to speak to them about their own salvation. Don't miss a moment to let your life shine!

– Shanna D. Gregor

*The nicest thing we can do for
our heavenly Father is to be kind
to one of His children.*

St. Teresa of Avila

HOSPITALITY

$\mathcal{L}$ord, I thank You for my home. Show my heart opportunities to open this home to others. I want to share what You've provided for me. As I practice hospitality, may Your love shine through my life. However my home compares with others, I thank You for what I have. I am grateful that Your Spirit is present here. Give me a generous, open heart, and use my home for Your good purposes.

~Jackie M. Johnson

And be kind to one another, tender-hearted, forgiving each other, just as God in Christ also has forgiven you.

Ephesians 4:32 NASB

Laughter and
Joy

And Sarah said, "God has made me laugh, and all who hear will laugh with me."

CONTAGIOUS LAUGHTER

Nothing brings more joy to our hearts than when God blesses our lives. Like Sarah, we may at first laugh with disbelief when God promises us our heart's desire. For some reason, we doubt that He can do what we deem impossible. Yet God asks us, as He did Sarah, "Is any thing too hard for the LORD?" (Genesis 18:14 KJV).

Then when the blessings shower down upon us, we overflow with joy. Everything seems bright and right with the world. With God, the impossible has become a reality. We bubble over with laughter, and when we laugh, the world laughs with us! It's contagious!

When Satan bombards us with lies—"God's not real"; "You'll never get that job"; "Mr. Right? He'll never come along"—it's time to look back at God's Word and remember Sarah. Imbed in your mind the truth that with God, nothing is impossible (see Matthew 19:26). And then, in the midst of the storm, in the darkness of night, in the crux of the trial, laugh, letting the joy of God's truth be your strength.

–Donna K. Maltese

It is pleasing to God whenever you rejoice or laugh from the bottom of your heart.

MARTIN LUTHER

JOY

*L*ord, You are my joy. Knowing You gives me gladness and strength. As my heart's shield, You protect and keep me from harm. Help me to face the future with joy. Fill me with Your good pleasures so I may bring enjoyment to my surroundings—at home, at work, and in my ministry. Help me to laugh more and smile often as I reflect on Your goodness. In Your presence, Lord, is fullness of joy.

~Jackie M. Johnson

*And even though you do not see [Jesus] now,
you believe in him and are filled with an
inexpressible and glorious joy, for you are receiving
the goal of your faith, the salvation of your souls.*

1 Peter 1:8–9 NIV

JOY IS JESUS

As children, we find joy in the smallest things: a rose in bloom, a ladybug at rest, the circles a pebble makes when dropped in water. Then somewhere between pigtails and pantyhose our joy wanes and eventually evaporates in the desert of difficulties.

But when we find Jesus, "all things become new" as the Bible promises, and once again we view the world through a child's eyes. Excitedly, we experience the "inexpressible and glorious joy" that salvation brings.

We learn that God's joy isn't based on our circumstances; rather, its roots begin with the seed of God's Word planted in our hearts. Suddenly, our hearts spill over with joy, knowing that God loves and forgives us and that He is in complete control of our lives. We have joy because we know this world is not our permanent home, and a mansion awaits us in glory.

Joy comes as a result of whom we trust, not in what we have. Joy is Jesus.

–Tina Krause

*Cheerfulness is the habit of
looking at the good side of things.*

W. B. Ullathorne

JOYFUL IN HOPE

*L*ord, I thank You for giving me hope. I don't know where I would be without You. I don't know what the future holds, but You give me the ability to be joyful even while I wait—even when I don't understand. Please help me to have a positive attitude and live with a mind-set of patience and courage as You work Your will in my life. Help me to remain faithful in prayer, Lord, and fully committed to You.

~Jackie M. Johnson

*My heart leaps for joy and I
will give thanks to him in song.*

PSALM 28:7 NIV

Nature

And seeing the multitudes, he went up into a mountain. . .and. . .his disciples came unto him: and he opened his mouth and taught them.

MATTHEW 5:1—2 KJV

God's Mountain Sanctuary

Melissa felt crushed beneath work, home, and church responsibilities. So much so, she could no longer give or listen, let alone hear from God. So she decided to take a day trip to the mountains to try to unwind.

There the forest hummed with a symphony of sound as beams of sunlight filtered through the vast timberland. As she strolled a wooded path, she noticed how God's creation kept perfect cadence with its Creator. No one directed the wildflowers to bloom, no one commanded the trees to reach upward, and no one forced the creek to flow downstream. No one but God, and nature simply complied.

Jesus often retreated to a mountain to pray. There He called His disciples to depart from the multitudes so that He could teach them valuable truths—the lessons we learn from nature. Don't fret: Obey God's gentle promptings and simply flow in the path He clears.

Do you yearn for a place where problems evaporate like the morning dew? Do you need a place of solace? God is wherever you are—behind a bedroom door, nestled alongside you in your favorite chair, or even standing at a sink full of dirty dishes. Come apart and enter God's mountain sanctuary.

- Tina Krause

All things bright and beautiful,
All creatures great and small,
All things wise and wonderful,
The Lord God made them all.

CECIL FRANCES ALEXANDER

A World in One Drop

O Lord, I have peered into a microscope and seen a world in one drop of water. I have gazed through a telescope and have seen stars and galaxies uncountable. When I see the majesty of Your vast creation, I am brought to my knees in wonder. But in my humble admiration, there is also a desperate question: Do You notice me and concern Yourself with me?

I thank You, Lord, for personally answering my question. When I am apprehensive, I put my trust in You, and You keep me safe. When I am lonely, You talk to me. When I am sad, You make me happy. When I am weak, I bow before You and feel Your strength.

– John Hudson Tiner

"You will go out in joy and be led forth in peace; the mountains and hills will burst into song before you, and all the trees of the field will clap their hands."

<small>Isaiah 55:12 NIV</small>

Nature Rejoices

The bumblebee-yellow float plane dropped off the young couple and their guide near a remote lake in the wilds of Alaska. It was their first Alaskan adventure vacation, and they expected to catch a lot of fish, but they hadn't realized how awestruck they would be as they drank in the majestic views that surrounded them. Standing in thigh-deep glacial waters, they cast their lines. A snowcapped volcano rose up on their left, and an ancient glacier reflected the sun on their right. The only sounds were those of nature itself—the rushing river, the wind in the trees, and an occasional whoop from the woman when she got a fish on her hook. They marveled at the pair of bald eagles that soared above them most of the day and the young bear that came out of the bush to investigate the strangers who had usurped his fishing rights.

We don't have to be outdoorsmen like our Alaska vacationers to appreciate and be inspired by the wonders of God's creation wherever we find ourselves. Wildflowers that grow alongside highways, a shed snakeskin—a found treasure that a boy brings to his mother—or the unusual cloud formations that dance in the sky before a storm inspire us to praise God, the Creator of all things. Nature declares the glory of the Lord.

–Austine Keller

For in the true nature of things,
if we will rightly consider, every
green tree is far more glorious than
if it were made of gold and silver.

MARTIN LUTHER

A Special Planet

*H*eavenly Father, the photographs of Earth taken from space always cause me to pause because of the stunning beauty they reveal: green forests, brown deserts, white clouds, and blue green oceans. The earth looks like a marvelous jewel set against the black background of space. It causes me to adore You, Lord, and remember You as the Creator.

Father, I appreciate the earth as Your special creation. Keep me alert to the goodness around me. But help me always be mindful that this earth is not my permanent home. Despite its beauty, the earth is but a way station to a much grander place with You. May I always live my life with the knowledge that heaven is my eventual destination.

~John Hudson Tiner

*"If God gives such attention to
the appearance of wildflowers—
most of which are never even seen—
don't you think he'll attend to you,
take pride in you, do his best for you?"*

Matthew 6:30 msg

Prayer

I call on you, O God, for you will answer me;
give ear to me and hear my prayer.

PSALM 17:6 NIV

AVAILABLE 24/7

No one is available to take your call at this time, so leave a message and we will return your call—or not—if we feel like it. . .and only between the hours of 4:00 and 4:30 p.m. Thank you for calling. Have a super day!

We've all felt the frustration of that black hole called voice mail. It is rare to reach a real, honest-to-goodness, breathing human being the first time we dial a telephone number.

Fortunately, our God is always available. He can be reached at any hour of the day or night and every day of the year—including weekends and holidays! When we pray, we don't have to worry about disconnections, hang-ups, or poor reception. We will never be put on hold or our prayers diverted to another department. The Bible assures us that God is eager to hear our petitions and that He welcomes our prayers of thanksgiving. The psalmist David wrote of God's response to those who put their trust in Him: "He will call upon me, and I will answer him" (Psalm 91:15 NIV). David had great confidence that God would hear his prayers. And we can, too!

-Austine Keller

You pay God a compliment by
asking great things of Him.

St. Teresa of Avila

THE DELIGHT OF
ANSWERED PRAYER

*L*ord, I thank You for the joy of answered prayer! You are amazing. I delight in You and thank You with a full heart. I asked and You answered. I receive what You give with a grateful heart. Lord, You are good. You are faithful. You are my joy and my delight. I praise Your holy name. I am smiling at You right now. Thank You for filling my heart with gladness, Lord.

~Jackie M. Johnson

Why are you downcast, O my soul?
Why so disturbed within me?
Put your hope in God, for I will yet
praise him, my Savior and my God.

PSALM 42:11 NIV

YET PRAISE HIM

Many individuals and prayer groups use the acronym ACTS to guide their prayers. The letters stand for Adoration, Confession, Thanksgiving, and Supplication. Note that adoration comes first, before the believer confesses sin, thanks God, or asks anything of Him. God delights in His children's praise and adoration.

If you have cared for a child, you have probably received genuine adoration at times as well as times of appreciation in response to something you have done for her or him. Which warms your heart more? Certainly it means more to be held in high esteem simply because of who you are in the child's life than to be told "I love you" when you hand out dollar bills or promise a trip to the zoo!

Imagine how God feels when one of His children praises Him simply for who He is, even when her circumstances are far from perfect. Don't you suppose it feels like a tight hug around His neck? A "just because" sort of hug, not the "I got something from you" sort.

Praise God regardless. Praise Him yet, as the psalmist did. Adore Him today, for He is God.

–Emily Biggers

We do not need to search for heaven over here or over there in order to find our eternal Father. In fact, we do not even need to speak out loud, for though we speak in the smallest whisper or the most fleeting thought, He is close enough to hear us.

St. Teresa of Avila

JOY IN PRAYING FOR OTHERS

*L*ord, I thank You for the joy and privilege of praying for others. What a blessing to be able to intercede, to stand in the gap and move heaven and earth for those I love. In all my prayers for those I know, may I have a heart of joy. Bless my family and friends, Lord. Bless those who need You today. May I find satisfaction in lifting up prayers for others.

– Jackie M. Johnson

In the morning, O Lord, you hear my voice; in the morning I lay my requests before you and wait in expectation.

PSALM 5:3 NIV

Rest and
Relaxation

*A twinkle in the eye means joy
in the heart, and good news
makes you feel fit as a fiddle.*

PROVERBS 15:30 MSG

How About Some Fun?

*H*ave you had any fun this week?"

This query, in and of itself, might sound odd, but two friends agreed to ask each other this question periodically because both had the tendency to plow through an entire week of school, work, church, and community commitments forgetting—or neglecting—to plan an activity or two for the sole purpose of recharging their own burnt-out batteries. Both women realized they would have to make an effort to carve out time for activities that brought them joy. For one, it was kayaking and hiking; for the other, it was settling into her favorite reading chair with a mystery novel.

God does not want His kids to be worn out and stressed out. He did not design us to be like little Energizer Bunnies that keep on going and going and going. We need time to recreate—to revive and refresh our bodies and minds. A little relaxation, recreation—and yes, fun—are essential components of a balanced life. Even Jesus and His disciples found it necessary to get away from the crowds and pressures of ministry to rest.

There's a lot of fun to be had out there—playing tennis or golf; jogging; swimming; painting; knitting; playing a musical instrument; visiting an art gallery; playing a board game; or going to a movie, a play, or a football game. Have you had any fun this week?

-Austine Keller

Relaxation was God's idea.

GINA MASELLI

NO NEED TO COUNT SHEEP

There are times, Lord, when I climb into bed, shut my eyes, and fall right to sleep. I wake up the next morning refreshed. There are other times, Lord, when the events of the day, the week, the month, follow me to bed and I lay there in turmoil. Lord, with You as my friend, how can I worry about my enemies? You constantly watch over me.

– Pamela Kaye Tracy

I pray that God, the source of hope, will fill you completely with joy and peace because you trust in him. Then you will overflow with confident hope through the power of the Holy Spirit.

ROMANS 15:13 NLT

GOD OF HOPE

In our busy, fast-paced lives, we may feel exhausted at times. Our culture fosters frenzy and ignores the need for rest and restoration. Constantly putting out fires and completing tasks, working incessantly, we may feel discouraged and disheartened with life. There is more to life than this, isn't there?

Our God of hope says, "Yes!" God desires to fill us to the brim with joy and peace. But to receive this gladness, rest, and tranquillity, we need to have faith in the God who is trustworthy and who says, "Anything is possible if a person believes" (Mark 9:23 NLT). We need to place our confidence in God who, in His timing and through us, will complete that task, mend that relationship, or do whatever it is we need. The key to receiving and living a life of hope, joy, and peace is recounting God's faithfulness out loud, quietly in your heart, and to others. When you begin to feel discouraged, exhausted, and at the end of your rope, stop; go before the throne of grace and recall God's faithfulness.

- Tina C. Elacqua

*Take rest; a field that has
rested gives a bountiful crop.*

OVID

Spiritual Health

L ord, I need Your times of refreshing in my life. Bread of Heaven, as You nourish my body with food, feed my soul with Your words of comfort and life. May I be filled with Your healing love, joy, and goodness. I praise You, Father, for providing green pastures, places to relax and unwind in the Spirit. Please still my heart from distractions and be the restorer of my soul.

–Jackie M. Johnson

Relax, everything's going to be all right;
rest, everything's coming together;
open your hearts, love is on the way!

JUDE 1 MSG

Simple
Pleasures

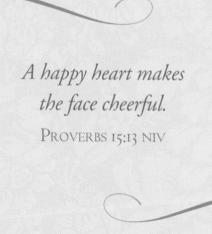

*A happy heart makes
the face cheerful.*

PROVERBS 15:13 NIV

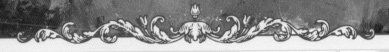

THE SECRET OF SERENDIPITY

Can you remember the last time you laughed in wild abandon? Better yet, when was the last time you did something fun, outrageous, or out of the ordinary? Perhaps it is an activity you haven't done since you were a child, like slip down a waterslide, strap on a pair of ice skates, or pitch a tent and camp overnight.

Women often become trapped in the cycle of routine, and soon we lose our spontaneity. Children, on the other hand, are innately spontaneous. Giggling, they splash barefoot in rain puddles. Wide-eyed, they watch a kite soar toward the treetops. They make silly faces without inhibition; they see animal shapes in rock formations. In essence, they possess the secret of serendipity.

A happy heart turns life's situations into opportunities for fun. For instance, if a storm snuffs out the electricity, light a candle and play games, tell stories, or just enjoy the quiet. When we seek innocent pleasures, we glean the benefits of a happy heart.

Jesus said, "I am come that they might have life, and that they might have it more abundantly" (John 10:10 KJV). God wants us to enjoy life, and when we do, it lightens our load and changes our countenance.

So try a bit of whimsy just for fun. And rediscover the secret of serendipity.

- Tina Krause

Into all our lives, in many simple,
familiar, homely ways, God infuses this
element of joy from the surprises of life,
which unexpectedly brightens our days
and fills our eyes with light.

HENRY WADSWORTH LONGFELLOW

FINDING CONTENTMENT

*L*ord, please help me to find my contentment in You. I don't want to be defined by "stuff"—the things I own or what I do. May my greatest happiness in life be knowing who You are and who I am in Christ. May I treasure the simple things in life, those things that bring me peace. With Your grace, I rest secure.

–Jackie M. Johnson

The earth and everything in
it belong to the Lord.

1 Corinthians 10:26 cev

COMFORT FOOD

A big mound of ice cream topped with hot fudge; a full bowl of salty, buttery popcorn; grilled cheese sandwiches and warm chicken noodle soup fixed by Mom—comfort food. There is nothing like a generous helping of things that bring the sensation of comfort to a worn body at the end of a long day or to a bruised mind after a disappointment. Those comfort foods soothe the body and mind because, through the senses, they remind us of happier and more secure times.

Romans 15:4 tells us that the scriptures are comfort food for the soul. They were written and given so that, through our learning, we would be comforted with the truths of God. Worldly pleasures bring a temporary comfort, but the problem still remains when the pleasure or comfort fades. However, the words of God are soothing and provide permanent hope and peace. Through God's Word, you will be changed, and your troubles will dim in the bright light of Christ. So the next time you are sad, lonely, or disappointed, before you turn to pizza, turn to the Word of God as your source of comfort.

~Nicole O'Dell